Poetic Outlets

Melica Niccole

Hampton Publishing House, LLC

Poetic Outlets was published by

Hampton Publishing House, LLC
P.O. Box 29201
Columbus, Ohio 43229

Copyright © 2007 by Melica Hampton

All rights reserved. This book may not be reproduced in any manner -without the written consent from the publisher.

Library of Congress Control Number: 2011927690
ISBN 978-0-9828745-1-6

Printed in the United States of America

Poems Written by

Melica Niccole

Edited by

Vian Yohn

Publishing Company

Hampton Publishing House, LLC

This book is dedicated
to the quiet people in the world,
who are more than the views and opinions of -others.
It is your time to shine
and show the world the -magnitude of your mind.

-Stay dedicated to your purpose in life.

Poems below were 1st published on Melica Niccole's Facebook Page:

Four- November 7, 2010

Passion- September 23, 2010

Act Like a Lady- December 20, 2009

MJ Poetic Song Flow- June 28, 2009

Melica Wants to Know- February 19, 2009

CHAPTERS

LIFE WAS NOT SUPPOSED TO BE THIS WAY

(6 poems; including My Life and Anger Management)

I AM MORE...

(12 poems; including So Addictive and Society's Child)

LOVE

(9 poems; including Love Was Supposed to be Everlasting)

THE OLDER AND NEW ME

(12 poems; including Mental Stimulation and Lost)

LIFE WAS NOT SUPPOSED TO BE THIS WAY

No Happiness

At a time like this,

How can I be happy?

Life has been taken away

And thrown right at me

My life is in shambles

Can't you see?

See the pain in my eyes

That's destined to be

To be the pain and suffering

That pains my heart

The ache in my heart

That's piercingly sharp

You still seem to wonder

Why I don't smile and shine

Because this world has been harsh

And very unkind

I can't take this life I live

I can't take it anymore

My happiness is gone

And destined to be more

No Car

He's upset

So there's no car for me

He won't return my calls

And he is dodging me

He doesn't want to pay for

The car I truly want

My thing is

He shouldn't have promised something

He really did not want

My Life

Stress and Depression

Are like my best friends

Showing up uninvited

Vowing to bring my life to an end

Taking my confidence

To an all-time low

Letting me feel a black woman's burden

Blow by blow

So addictive and enticing

As in those who welcome sin

Releasing special kinds of endorphins

Which takes the madness in

My emotions are uncontrollable

Like my words, which flow right out

Rarely thinking twice

Before my words take someone out

What great best friends

Stress and depression have come to be

Showing off my talents

Of being someone I despise

Oh, look

It's me

Grumpy

My co-workers said I'm grumpy

Well...

Maybe it's true

My grumpiness seems to reveal itself

When I've been awakened

A time or two

When I'm breaking

And at times

Need time to myself

You touch me

Awaken me

Hoping there will be nothing but happiness in me

How can I be happy

When you have disturbed my peace?

Now I'm in a place

Where sleep must cease

What kind of person are you?

To take away such a beautiful thing

Wake me from my slumber

Point to my finger and say

"Oh, what a beautiful ring"

Your statement could have waited

Until I woke up again

Now I have an attitude

Which doesn't want to end

Many Faces

Evil wears many disguises

It is the one who it overshadows

Who it despises

The pity of one

Is the one who is blinded

Blinded by the dark

For the blinded could not find it

Evil is as evil does

For truthful and honest

It never was

Quick and charming

For that's the game

Leading you

To its terrain

Anger Management

It is an art form that some cannot comprehend

Too focused on bending the spoon

Not realizing

It is the brain that must bend

Over analyzing every situation

Never missing a chance to bicker

At any occasion

Livid emotions and fist of stone

Experiencing things to the mind unknown

Capitalizing on reputation

In order to not look like a fool

Enlightenment for the soul

Takes you from fool

To someone who has been schooled

Self-control, unity of the mind,

And a host of other things

Asserting yourself

And evaluating the things your life will bring

Tranquility sets in

And the renaissance of the mind begins

Providing lessons for new travelers to transcend

I AM MORE

Deadly Venom

They call me Ms. Poison

For I breathe a deadly venom

Infecting the world

As if I was

Influenza

My eyes tell a story

That my thoughts cannot comprehend

Is your brain on loan?

For these brothers need one to lend

Can you not hear

The words that I bluntly speak?

Or should I abash your character

Is that what you seek?

Do my words overwhelm you

To the point of no control?

Maybe you should start small

And put your vocabulary on birth control

My poison is deadly

It's the number one killer

It sends chills through your spine

As if it was a thriller

I'm screaming at the top of my lungs

I'm the deadliest of all morbidities

I'm the word called Lust

Was that hard for you to see?

I Am...

I am versatile

When I talk

I don't have to talk really loud

I can talk softly

However, my voice can be heard for many miles

I don't have to put on a show

Like the girls on *Girls Gone Wild*

Like Luther Vandross

I only have to worry about

The *Here and Now*

I am calm

My personality soothes the raging heart

As calm as the Red Sea

That many centuries ago

Moses parted

So tranquil that

I have people amazed before I even start

I am powerful

The knowledge that I withhold is deadly

Some of my words

Are capable of beheading me

I embrace my heritage

For many are unable to see

The past, the pain

Which lead them to be

I am woman

I am versatile, calm, powerful and sweet

I bring the unity

For which you seek

I am a great listener

For I know you have a story to tell

I am courteous

And I mediate well

I know you know me

For there is one in every family

However this is the only time

You really took a look at me

So Addictive

My personality is so addictive

Attracting uniqueness

That makes you want to get with this

I'm funny

And yes,

I'm sweet

Have your heart palpitating

Souls mingling and relating

Those unlike me start the hating

Master minds contemplating

You don't believe the words I speak

Confidence

Is that what you seek?

You need to bandage your character

Change your status

From a pro to an amateur

I represent the big leagues

Move aside

And don't hinder me

Let my soul shine like the sun beams

Glaring and overpowering

Rip your spirit from your body at the seams

In my eyes, I speak the truth

Kindness doesn't lie

I'm the living proof

You still want to doubt my persona

Thinking I'm a show-off

I'm no prima donna

I give it to you delightfully

Hardly ever will you see

The spite in me

My soul will forever stay shining

Attracting other souls

That takes on the crippling disorder of pining

Let me

Give you a personality signing

Autograph your disposition

Is there something I forgot to mention?

Time to smile at you

You're my invention

Stop

Take a bow

End of

The expedition

My Scent

Brothers breathe my scent

And think they know the fragrance

Unaware that my perfume goes through many changes

The scent is sweet and strong at times

And with time, intoxicating like fine wine

A scent capable of stimulating the mind

A scent so sweet that it entangles the body

And begins to bind

And then the twist begins and the scent has evolved

Mysterious to all of those involved

The scent is now dull and really not sweet

It's trying to catch the rhyme, but it misses a beat

People begin to wonder

If the first scent was just a fake

If the aroma it released

Was just a mistake

But did they stop to wonder

That the scents were intertwined?

Overtaken by the body, released by the mind

!

I speak honestly

A lie is something that you don't have to worry about from me

I tell the truth

Even when you don't want to hear me

My words are lucid

As an adult

I have never been a nuisance

I get along with most crowds

From time to time

I seem to wonder how

I am unbreakable

Highly motivated

Rarely incapable

I possess the key

Going to be

All that I

Can be

I am me

I am proud

I am black

I am woman

I am

I am a proud black woman

Once Upon a Time

If only it was that easy

Once upon a time

If only once there came a time

That I could say

Once upon a time

I'd throw my head back

(ha)

Because has there ever been a time?

A time I could end my story

With happily ever after

A time where life's situations

Could start in laughter

My once upon a time

Has been trivialized

By fantasies of tropical skies

Sitting on the beach sipping

Ice tea of the Island Long

While listening to that song

Something about seeing nothing wrong

While people start recognizing their Sex on the Beach

Leave a message after the beep for no one is able to be reached

My head begins to turn as men yell "Hey, Bahama Mama"

Looking at the other women

For I want

No more drama

Because once upon a time

There was a time

There came a time

That my once upon a time

Could be real

And sublime

Mysterious

My life is such a mystery

Like people quoting quotes

Quoting folks

But can't quote their own history

I walk through a maze

Unable to see

Blinded by the tree

But character can't be displaced

I practice what I preach

For if I don't practice the preaching

My mind will overlook the teachings

Those in which I seek

I'm a great teller of stories

For it's the pride land

That makes the man

Where Denzel shall get his <u>GLORY</u>

I reap what I sow

For the wind blows many ways

Many days

Not leaving many places to go

I'm creative and unique

From poetry to painting

Designing, it's amazing

All the things my mind keeps

I end so delightfully

People think I'm that type you see

Quiet and shy

Not realizing the hype in me

Sophisticated Lady

I'm so sophisticated

Lyrics are underrated

Age always debated

Ma, look how I made it

Skills accentuated

People, you got to hate it

Especially those that I dated

I got to be elated

I'm all sensual

Just to let you know

Listen to my flow

1, 2, uh, here I go

Boy, you know that I'm smooth

Like Stella who got her groove

Back then and made a move

Old school teaching new school

My style is so nice

Make you think once, then twice

My mind is so suffice

Got you paying the price

My words are so true

Now what you want to do

Take you to Peru

Make you lose your coo'

But that's just who I am

My aura makes you want to jam

My character is that deal

Because I keep it real

Now you know who I am

And why I make you jam

And why I am debated

I'm so sophisticated

Society's Child

Raised by a mother

Who was so diligent in her craft

So unique and specific

You wouldn't want to cross her path

She molded me

And gave me what she thought I needed

Even gave a detailed sketch

Of my goals

To make sure I succeeded

She did this for all her children

For she was the keeper of societal success

She believed she had the key

And following her,

You would surely be blessed

What she failed to realize is that

Every child goes through different things

That you have to follow your heart

And what life brings

That sometimes society's norm

Is so abstract

And once you do something out of the norm

Red flags go up

And people begin to turn their backs

My mother is so powerful

In what she believes

But sometimes you have to watch her

For she, too, deceives

She paints a pretty picture

Of beautiful doves and blue skies

Deep black hair and baby brown eyes

The moon fading as the sun begins rise

New born births and souls beginning to die

My mother is the societal mistress

Intentions overshadowed

Overpowered

And placed in an abyss

Attitude

Don't mistake attitude for anger

For if you do

Your mind has been conditioned

And in the mist of being in danger

A woman's attitude

Can exude

Confidence and sexiness

Strong and

Overpowering

Like a sweet and delicate kiss

She walks into a room

And everyone starts to stare

Is it the scent of her perfume

Or the way she flicks her hair?

Is it the gleam in her eyes

Or the way she smiles at you?

Leaving you

Amazed and mesmerized

Not knowing exactly what to do

No,

It's the way

She carries herself

The way she swaggers

And keeps good health

Her walk is like a cannon

Ready to explode

It's compelling

Giving you thoughts of her to hold

What is it about her

That keeps you staring?

It's her attitude

How it's sweet and daring

Phases of a Personality

My personality is alluring

Illness-eradicating, curing

Increased-life-expectancy-assuring

It's so inviting

Soothing poetry writing

Sunny days on the way, let's go kiting

Sitting in a rocking chair, relaxing

It is loving

Warm bodies and sweet hugging

Friendly smiles and familiar tugging

Sweet whisperings in the ear, saying nothing

It is euphoric

An energizing, boost-providing kick

The oomph that speeds up your heart and makes it tick

The antidote that keeps your body from getting sick

It is the power of the soul

The things that make you glow

The gestures he will never know

The way the story unfolds

It is my personality

Mysterious to those who are not me

One gatekeeper has the key

Let the story be told

It is me

Out of the Darkness

Out of the darkness

Into the light

Into God's hands

Where His blessings wraparound me tight

Thank You LORD

For You have blessed me

Gave me light

To enable me to see

You have stayed with me

Through hard times

Through happy times

Giving me peace of mind

You are my savior

The brightness to the sky

The reason why

It's hard for me to lie

I thank Thee for

All You have done for me

And look forward

To all the goodness You will dispense from me

LOVE

Soul Searching

My soul has been searching

For a soul similar to mine

A soul so captivating

That it embraces and slows time

It attracts me

Without having to push

Showing me the true meaning of love

And giving me an adrenaline rush

It is the epitome of a true soul mate

Gets along with most people

And wards off hate

Honesty comes easily

For he does not want to hurt me

In tune with the Lord

Because he wants to better me

Being in a relationship with him

Means loyalty

He loves me for me

And does not want to change me

Black and Puerto Rican

He told me he was black and Puerto Rican

And that I was what he was seeking

That in tongues I would be speaking

And like a fiend I would be tweaking

That he wanted me to be his

In his heart is where I would live

Kids he wanted 2 to 3

And he wanted me for me

That he wanted to make love

Under the stars

And he wanted to travel with me

To Pluto and Mars

That he wanted my soul

To be engulfed in his

And that he would give me whatever I wanted

Because he was my very own *Wiz*

That our lives were so alike

And a man like him

Would do me right

That he would make my heart skip a beat

And he would pamper me from head to feet

That his word is the truth

And that his love is 100% proof

My mind was so amazed

All the things this dude would say

And like Burger King, "I could have it my way"

And this streamed from 2 talks

And the papers I should subpoena my man to walk

And that he was more than just talk

He was the destination

Amid

The endless walk

Love was Supposed to be Everlasting

Love was supposed to be everlasting,

But a love like this is worth passing

I'm emotionally disturbed

I can't pronounce the word

Let alone the verb

I feel like my world is unwinding

I'm denying

And can't stop from crying

You blinded me

Promised me the world

While you bound me

Tied my legs together

And insulted me

Could this be?

My downfall came so suddenly

Oh,

Now you want to cuddle with me

But have you heard,

"Wait long, wait wrong"?

I waited too long

And as I waited

I heard the same sad song

You sang so sweet in the introduction

Now your lyrics

Are what make me unable to function

I waited wrong

It was wrong for me to take your lies

I despise

The way you hindered me and covered my eyes

You made me believe that I was the one for you

Who knew?

That you would do me like you do

Making me think that I was more than your one-hit wonder

Your sun in the mist of thunder

Now it's over just like the summer

But I'm to blame

I gave you all of me

Including the fame

I let you see my soul unleashed

My trust you breached

Now you're trying to hold on like a leech

That's not happening

Because love was supposed to be everlasting

Not controlling, vindictive, unworthy, worth passing

Love once was … everlasting

The One

Liking you is complicated

For I try so hard

To keep my composure

And my feelings afar

You have touched a spot in my soul

Given me something good to hold

Something so beautiful and bold

A life that I wouldn't mind when turns old

I love the way you look at me

The way you touch my skin

The way you make me want you

The way you laugh and grin

You are sexy and smooth

Appropriate for every mood

Worthy of being my boo

You are

A dream come true

Love

Love is a joy

An overwhelming explosion of emotions

A scent

That can't be labeled Love Number 9 Potion

An unconscious action

That speaks louder than words

A heart

Which does not want to be left undisturbed

A fragment

Of the intensity my body holds

A mind

In which society constantly molds

A face

To whom I pledge my heart

A hand

In which the body is the whole and the hand is the part

Love is and will always be

A part of you

A part of me

I'm Sorry

Sorry that your best isn't good enough

That my love starts off sweet

Then gets a little rough

I'm sorry

That my love deep inside

Makes me do strange things

And I want to run away and hide

I'm sorry

For the good times

The bad times

The times I cry

The times I ask God

WHY?

Why do my emotions

Overcloud my judgment

Making it hard for me to focus

This is just so bogus

I had always vowed to be that person

To not get trapped by love

And then start cursing

Showing off in front of your friends

I wasn't that type of person

This is something I knew

I was certain

But it wasn't me

It was the burden

The burden that love had placed on my heart

The burden of love disappearing and taking my heart

The burden of love making me look like a fool

Because everyone knows that looking like a fool

Just isn't cool

But I have to reiterate my point

I'm sorry

I'm sorry for the...

Everlasting, uncontrollable, quick to react, insenstive

Always looking for a reason, jealous, egotistical, righteous, always right,

Argumentative, loving, caring, that's my boo, love that I have for you

As I end my saga

I just want to say

I'm sorry

Ize

I fantasize

I visualize

Your soul

Uniting with mine

I'm hypnotized

I realize

That I love

Your brown eyes

I cannot lie

I even sigh

When you are sad

I ask God why

I exercise

I am so wise

That I would love

This special guy

Your soul will rise

Do not despise

Open your soul

And let it flow

There's love for you

Within my eyes

I just thought

That you should know

I Can Breathe

I can breathe now

Finally,

I am free

And I will show you how

I take the breath through my lungs

And exhale it out

I can breathe so efficiently

That I want to shout it out

I am free of all the burdens

And the controlling things

I am free of the cursing

And the unhappy beings

My curse has been lifted

So please make way

Because like me

You will be able to breathe

Someday

My Love

My love is like a dove

Flying through the sky

Taking to the air

As grace begins to fly

Moving steadfastly

Exploring the firmament

Having people take notice and stating

"It must be heaven-sent"

It is a love

That cannot be taken away

It will be around

Noon, night, and throughout the day

My love is only for you

And you should know

That when life is gone

My love will never go

THE OLD, NEW ME

Passion

Some people say they have the passion to make dreams come true

While waiting for a lifeline

Is it phone a friend?

50/50?

No, it's called about time

It's about the time that you let your passion

Seep through the soles of your shoes

Now click your heels like *Dorothy*

Because there's no place like home

Home

Home of the brave

Home of the free

Home where passion lives brilliantly

Alicia Wiggins speaks of *A Place Like Home*

A place like home

A place like home

A place where in the dwellings and cracks of the impossible

Hard work shuns away those without the drive to start the ignition

It's not impossible

The possibilities lie in those ready to take the journey

Ready to make a way

Ready to endure the struggle and pain

Passion has made its way into everyone's life

It embellishes those who live by its word

And lie dormant in those without the light

Act Like a Lady

You tell me to...

Walk like a lady

Talk like a lady

Take my legs and cross like a lady

Eat like a lady

Sleep like a lady

Make a poem to be like a lady

But your words have focused on my visual commitments to exemplify I'm a

woman

You tell me to be a woman, but when my emotions and tenderness show I'm a

woman

You ignore the very thing that makes my heart bleed

You ignore my voice of expression

Because my emotions are something you don't need

You make me feel as though I have exaggerated the feelings I carry deep inside

But maybe you have underestimated the feelings you try to hide

Why can't you make up your mind?

Because if I don't show these feelings

Then I'm considered heartless

A useless human being who sits dazed by this world and its

TO BE A WOMAN COMMANDMENTS

If you knew how to be a woman,

Then why are you still amazed at the acts of women these days?

I can't put women into a category because women aren't all the same

I mean, we all are considered women, but

We're not all the same

We don't dress the same

Speak the same

Enter love or friendships the same

We don't cook the same

Smell the same

"BETCHA BY GOLLY WOW"

We're not the same

So next time you start your proclamation with

"Why do women…"

You may want to rephrase your statement

To "why do women I date, come in contact with, or like

Do these certain things?"

Melica Wants to Know...

Melica wants to know

When spring has sprung

And life has begun

And the world is less bitter

And everyone can call themselves a winner

Will the hope be restored?

Will there be a cure for the poor?

Will the health of this country move more into a socialized health system?

Or will our health be victimized like in the movie *Sicko*?

Will we be thrown out of our hospital beds

For a fee we cannot pay?

Left on the side of the curb

Because in darkness we cannot find our way

Heroes from 9/11 tragedy

Suffering from respiratory diseases, for health insurance is what they lack

But they didn't lack the stamina when those planes chose to attack

What's wrong with the State of our Union

For the address we did not receive

The address was like a foreign policy

One which most could not conceive

The health of this country continues to make us different

Among other varying factors

Some people have insurance

Some people don't

Some people will get health services

Some people won't

That's the brutal reality

That we must face

Because some of us will be the percentage of the population

That will be stuck in the waiting room, waiting

Overlooked not because the deadly injury we have obtained

But for the lack of insurance we have maintained

Sickly souls whose pride has been exposed

Inability to have health and the outcome rubbed in our nose

This message is critical

At this point in life

I have to be cynical

People are suffering

Life holding on by a thread

Pull the cord

She can't pay her bill

That's what the doctor said

Was this world created to profit off of people's sickness

Sometimes it's really hard for me to get this

Home of the brave and land of the free

But free doesn't mean health services for you and me

Free to roam this world unconsciously knowing

That if I die today I don't know where my body will be going

For if I have no health insurance, what am I to do?

Sit on my couch until my body and soul turn blue?

Watch life pass me by because sometime in life I am destined to die?

But I just sigh

Then ask, why?

Why am I predestined to be the earliest to die?

MJ Poetic Song Flow

He called her *Dirty Diana*

As he moon walked all over her heart

She couldn't believe her ears

Because he promised her

They would never part

His words cut like a knife

As he told her *Beat It*

This is my ultimatum

So take it or leave it

Her soul was crushed

Because she used to be his *Pretty Young Thing*

She was the *Butterflies* in his stomach

And the notes that made his heart sing

She went from being Anna Jean

In a matter of moments

To his very own *Billie Jean*

She felt like he was *Bad*

And he really knew it.

He gave her to the count of 3

To disappear and show it.

This is a *Thriller*

She told herself

To take away the pain

For it was only yesterday

"*I Want to Rock with You*"

Was the verse he sang

The song of his choice used to be

The Way You Make Me Feel

But the feeling is no more

How will she ever deal?

He is no longer her *Man in the Mirror*

He has taken a new trail

All you can ask her is

"Annie, are you Ok? Annie, are you Ok? Are you Ok, Annie?

She's been hit by, she's been struck by a *Smooth Criminal*"

All I can say is it's *Human Nature*

To fall in and out of love

And ask your lover

"*Do You Remember the Time* when we fell in love?

Or when you told me

I'll Be There?"

There are no *ABC*s to love

This is so unfair

Annie wants to be in love because to her

There's no *Black or White*

She wants to say to him

"*Don't Stop Till You Get Enough*

Because *You Rock My World*"

But it's a little too late

For love could not wait

The heart stopped beating rampantly

The body fatigued instantly

The mind faded suddenly

And MJ will live on forever

Four

We are four

Four women

Four beautiful women ripped from the same womb

Grabbing at the walls of opportunity

Wanting to take the safe route

But not wanting the consequences of the journey

Four women

Four women who say the same "I can do bad all by myself" quote

But live by different "I can do bad all by myself" standards

Four women

I emphasize that four

Like it was the last of my mama's dreams

That she held to the highest standards

Dreams that she would not let slip right through the tips of her fingers

Because she believed so much in these dreams

That she would die, fighting for the life of them

Four women

Entering life

Sprinting toward the finish line of unconditional happiness

Fighting the exhaustion developing in our bodies

For fatigue we can get over

But defeat

We cannot

Though sometimes we stumble

And lie very still

We learn from our downfall

And strengthen our will

We know who we are

And always stay true

We are the product of our mama

And know what we need to do

Mental Stimulation

I want to make

Mental love to you

I want to speak the language

Only known by souls of like caliber

Engaging in unspoken dialect

That will make Egyptian Goddesses

Protect this union of cognitive stimulation

The words that protrude from your lips

Immediately attack my nervous system

Leaving my spine in a state of…

Satisfaction

My body cannot take the

Release of endorphins

That travel at an expeditious speed

Making my emotions rage with fulfillment

From the intuitiveness of our connection

The linkage has been made

I don't want to tell you this is

Something that it's not

Or something that it probably is

My thought processes

Have not been able to rationalize

What I think it should be

Because I may overanalyze

A simple union of intellectuals

That was destined to meet

Share life experiences

With afterthoughts of…

Have I met this person before?

I know this is the

First time that I

Sat down and spoke with this individual, but does my

Soul recognize the spirit of him who sits before me

The spirit of such divine confidence

And strength

That his brain interlocks with mine

Like a jigsaw puzzle

Connecting the sagittal suture

To the lambdoid suture

Does he possess the power to free my mind

Of thoughts that people just want someone to listen to them?

That knowledge is power

But nothing unless the receiver

Is receptive to receive

The insight that was given

I must come up for air

But air has seeped through my visual image of you

That I

Sit here like a deer caught in the headlights of a perfect beam

That talks to me and tells me to leave all my worries down by the river bend

The beam is so magnificent that it tells me to stay

Right in the peripherals of those who spend all their lives talking

But really not saying much

It tells me to give in to it

For there is nothing greater

Than the connection of two

That feels like one

But if my

Words didn't speak to you like the

Pen that spoke to this paper

I just have to realize that

I'm....

Mentally

Physically

Emotions reacted chemically

Stimulated

Infatuated

By your

Soul

Lost

Lost

Unfound to those who pass without regard to the things that happen for a -

Reason

Those who live so exuberantly

That they lack the knowledge to know they are in the presence of...

Greatness

Treasure that has been hidden from the world to see

For the world might damage its rarity

Scarce

Hidden treasure that not even Indiana Jones can dig up and prove he holds such

Treasures captive

Lost

A feeling of disconnection from all that moves around freely

All that plagues the inside of ears and ruptures emotions,

Which produces a steam-enveloping body of burnt promises

Promises that embed in the mind

Like a surgically implanted microchip

That locates broken promises with remnants of bad attitudes as the result

Burnt attitudes

Which cast off a stench worse than an overnight stay at the finest landfill in the

City

Finest garbage that slides off the tongue and slithers through the teeth

Because garbage has been accepted as the new truth

You ask

Why am I lost?

Because truth is the information that is becoming so obsolete

That those who speak it

Are overwhelmed by those who want to be it the presence of it.

Let not my truth

Bring about the raptures of the swarming honey bees that feed on my

Sweetly coated nectar

That it drains the life from up out of me

I'm lost

Nowhere to be found

Unable to digest the oxygen that wants to flow down my trachea

In a sprint to reach my lungs

Because there is a devastating need for the connection of oxygenated blood

To move freely throughout my body and release the most powerful energy

That yearns to be emancipated...

Carbon dioxide

I'm lost

In search of a way

In search for the light that shines brighter than the brightest beam

Carrying a moon princess and her team serene

In search

Searching for the presence

That magnifies my spirit in a way

That I sit hypnotized at the poetic structure of the misconstrued

I lose myself

Lost in translation that I'm considerably called

The Lost

Quiet

I'm not quiet

Though I sit here

Bottled up like a mime who's been thinking

Way too long

My mind dissects the statement

As if I am an anatomy student

Dissecting a fascia covered cadaver

With intentions to reveal

Something that's hidden beneath

All the muscles

Bulging

Ready to pop

And divulge what lies underneath.

Me

Though I know

Cradled inside my soul

Lies an unconditioned character

Who trails no one's words

Believes no such truths

And tells no such tales

This same individual spirit

Has the luxury of not being robbed by the illusions of society's misconceptions

And thinks in a manner that is trivial to most

I sit

Dormant in reality

For if I interact with the ill-mannered

My words will be thrashed by the spiteful

And swallowed by the vindictive

But you know what

I sit here

Quiet

Talking to no one

Engaging in no conversations

Independent of all my own thoughts

Because I get no pleasure in connecting with

Those who soak in the creamy stench of relational gossip

I am an independent thinker

Uncle Jack-A-Lack

This is the

Beginning of the end

Of a

Life that will transcend

From

Reminiscing about a life

That was blessed with kids and a wife

To the words that caressed our souls

Because the depth of our love,

He will always know

He stood by our sides

Said, "Girlie, that's a hoop ride."

And "my hair is naturally curly,

Because I got that good stuff,

All I need is water to slick it up."

He gave out money for good grades

And promised he had Chico DeBarge good waves

He smiled and laughed so delightfully

And was always ready to put up a fight for me

He lived his life to the fullest

Smiling

Laughing

Enjoying

And saying I LOVE YOU

Helpful

Handy

Silly

Because he was that coo'

Now, I

Stand here before you

To wish Robert Phalo A.K.A. Junkyard A.K.A. Uncle Jack-A-Lack

A farewell

And goodbye, too

Rhythm & Blues

My rhythm is my blues

I strive for perfection

Like an artist who shines shoes

Who am I to say

That your work isn't cool?

I think I would be a

Damn fool

To stand here

And devalue you

My blues to my rhythm

Speaks magnitudes of cadenced

Eruptions

I sway because my blues

Send chills

From looks, stares, and

Just by you touching

I'm metaphorically in tune

With my emotions

Like

My heart has been victimized and

Run over by 1,000 Egyptian kings

My happiness has been enslaved

And threatened, "This is Why the Caged Bird Sings"

I sing

Because my rhythm brings about a poise

That no one can take away

My rhythm

Is my character

That no matter how hard people try

They just can't seem to break away

From

No longer will I sit amongst the shy and timid

Because

I have something to say

No longer will your voice overpower me

Because

This is my day

I say

My rhythm is my blues

My blues are my rhythm

And without both of these working together

I would be spastic, obsessed, and unconvinced

Rhythm less blues

Masterpieces

Most people live their lives

Being a created version of what they thought they should have been

Nothing but a fabricated part of their imagination

That plagues the thoughts of others like them

They sip so sweetly

On the freshly brewed grounds of the unknown

The taste is like no other

That they wake up ever so early in the morning

To watch the drippings fuse together

And create a masterpiece

The masterpiece which stands before them is vibrant with colors that

Sashay across the eye of the beholder

To exude a confidence that was meant to stand apart

But has been thrust in a crowd of like masterpieces

The intent was to be unique

But uniqueness has transcended to become more of a trend

That leaves everyone looking like cloned iconic photocopied pictures

Ask yourself

Are you a picture?

Better Days Ahead

I know there are better days ahead

Because that's what GOD really said

He said He had

You in His heart

That His love for you

Would never part

Believe in me

Like I believe in you

Let God prevail

That's all you have to do

I know it's hard

And you want to give up

But don't give in

Just step it up

He believes in you

And sees the glow in your heart

Keep the light shinning

And He will surely do His part

Referenced Material

Anger Management (Poem)

Wachowski, A (Director). (1999) The Matrix [Motion Picture].

Back of Book Cover (Poetic Outlets)

Hampton, H. (Director). (1987) Eyes on the Prize [TV Series].

Black & Puerto Rican (Poem)

Burger King (2011). Retrieved April 6, 2010, from Burger King website: http://www.bk.co

I Am (Poem)

Girls Gone Wild (1997-2011). Retrieved April 6, 2010, from Girls Gone Wild page: http://www.girlsgonewild.com

Van dross, L. (Song Writer/Performer). (2003) Radio City Music Hall. [Music].

Lost (Poem)

Sato, J. (Director). (1995-2000) Sailor Moon [-TV Series]

Spielberg, S. (Director). (1989) Indiana Jones and the Last - Crusade. [Motion Picture].

West, K. (Song Writer/Performer). (2010) My Dark Twisted -

Fantasy [Music].

Love (Poem)

Launer, D (Director). (1992) Love Potion Number 9 [Motion-Picture].

Melica Wants to Know

Moore, M (Director). (2007) Sicko [Motion Picture].

Mysterious (Poem)

Zwick, E (Director). (1989) Glory [Motion Picture].

MJ Poetic Song Flow (Poem)

Jackson, M. (Song Writer/Performer). (1982, 2008) Thriller 25 [Music].

Jackson, M. (Song Writer/Performer). (1984, 2003) Michael Jackson Number Ones [Music].

The Jackson 5. (Performers). (2000) Jackson 5 Gold [Music].

Passion (Poem)

Fleming, V (Director). (1939) The Wizard of Oz [Motion Picture].

Key, F.S. (Composer). (1814) The Star Spangled Banner [Music].

Motown & Universal Pictures (Producers). (1978) The Wiz [-Motion Picture].

Passion (Poem)- continued

The Stylistics (2000). The Best of the Stylistics [Music].

Wiggins, Alicia. (2009) A Place Like Home: Indigo.

Rhythm & Blues (Poem)

Angelou, M. (2009) Why the Caged Bird Sings: Random House.

Sophisiticated Lady (Poem)

Sullivan, K (Director). (1998) How Stella Got Her Grove Back [Motion Picture].

Poetic Outlets was brought to you by the creative talents of

Melica Niccole

Follow the author at MelicaNiccole.com,

Twitter.com/MelicaNiccole,

&

MelicaNiccolesRealmofCreativity.blogspot.com

Look for other titles by Melica

such as:

Dead Wrong

Coming Soon:

Unleashing My Poetic Soul

All in Together Girls

Jacob (Sequel to Dead Wrong)

Hampton Publishing House, LLC can be contacted at

P.O. Box 1254* Union, NJ 07083*

Visit the company website at

www. HamptonPublishingHouse.com

Make reading an essential part of your daily activities

www.ingramcontent.com/pod-product-compliance
Lightning Source LLC
Chambersburg PA
CBHW032021040426
42448CB00006B/691